CONTENTS

OUT OF THIS WORLD

Carole Stott

WALKER BOOKS
AND SUBSIDIARIES

LONDON · BOSTON · SYDNEY

1

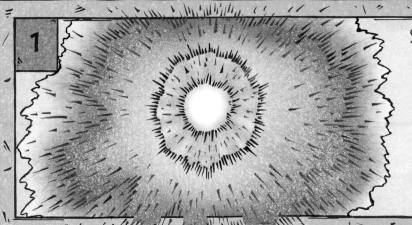

Scientists who study the universe are called astronomers. They believe that it began 15,000 million years ago, in a huge explosion called the Big Bang.

2 The Big Bang explosion was so powerful that it hurled super-hot gas out in every direction. And that's all there was to the universe at first — gas. Slowly, the gas cooled and formed into clouds. Then, after hundreds of millions of years, stars began to form in the clouds.

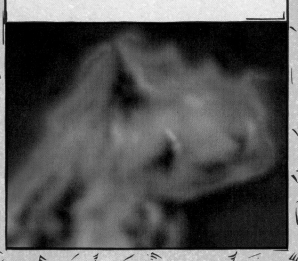

4

3 The universe is always changing. Stars live for millions of years, but even they eventually grow old and die. New stars are being born all the time, though, and sometimes planets form around them, too.

And although the Big Bang happened thousands of millions of years ago, the force of the explosion was so strong that the stars are still moving outwards today. So the universe is spreading and getting bigger all the time!

2 THE UNIVERSE

BIGGER AND BIGGER

1 The universe is everything — you, your home, and everything around you.

2 It's the whole Earth and everything on it, and the Sun and the Moon, too.

3 But that's just for starters. The Earth is only one of...

4 ...nine planets that travel around the Sun. The others are Mercury, Venus, Mars, Jupiter, Saturn, Uranus, Neptune and Pluto — and most of these planets have moons of their own, as well.

6 And our Solar System is just one small part of a vast star-group, called a galaxy. All of the stars you see at night belong to our galaxy. We call it the Milky Way.

SOLAR SYSTEM

SUN

Mercury

Venus

Earth

Mars

Jupiter

Saturn

Uranus

Neptune

Pluto

WE ARE HERE

MILKY WAY

WE ARE HERE

5 Along with our star, the Sun, this family of planets and moons is called the Solar System. And it's huge — from edge to edge, the Solar System measures about 15 million million kilometres.

7 There are also lots of other stars that you can't see in the Milky Way. Astronomers think there are about 200,000 million stars in our galaxy, and that like our Sun, some of them have planets.

4 THE UNIVERSE

8 The Milky Way isn't the only galaxy in the universe, though. Some of those fuzzy patches of light you see in the sky at night are actually other galaxies — far, far away in space.

10 But the universe doesn't stop there. Our Local Group is just one of several other clusters in a group known as the Local Supercluster. And superclusters are the biggest things in the universe!

LOCAL GROUP

WE ARE HERE

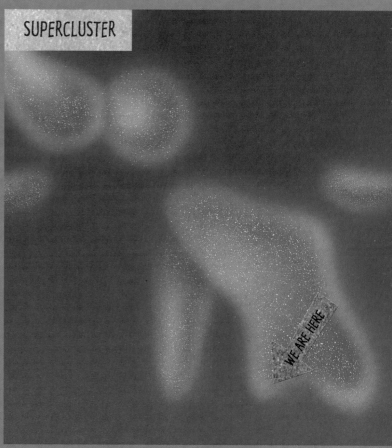

SUPERCLUSTER

WE ARE HERE

9 And even these galaxies are only part of a much bigger group which astronomers call a cluster. The Milky Way belongs to a cluster known as the Local Group, which has about 30 other galaxies.

11 In fact, the universe is so mind-bogglingly big that astronomers think that you'd need a tape-measure 300 million million million million kilometres long to measure it!

THE UNIVERSE 5

TRAVELLING LIGHT

1 Distances in space are far too big for astronomers to measure with tape-measures, of course.

2 One of the things astronomers use instead is a laser — a machine that sends out a very narrow, incredibly powerful beam of light.

1 The Moon is so far away that it would take over 140 days to travel there by car. But the Moon is actually our closest neighbour — most things in space are much, much further away.

2 You wouldn't want to drive to the Andromeda Galaxy, for example. It's the nearest galaxy to us, yet it's 21 million million million kilometres away!

3 This laser beam is being fired at the Moon to measure how far away it is. When the beam hits the Moon's surface, it will bounce straight back down to Earth.

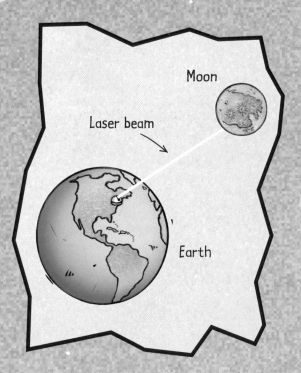

Moon

Laser beam

Earth

4 Astronomers know that light travels at 300,000 kilometres a second. So they just need to halve the time it takes for a laser beam to go to the Moon and bounce back.

5 As a laser beam takes just over two seconds to do this, astronomers have worked out that the Moon is about 384,000 kilometres away.

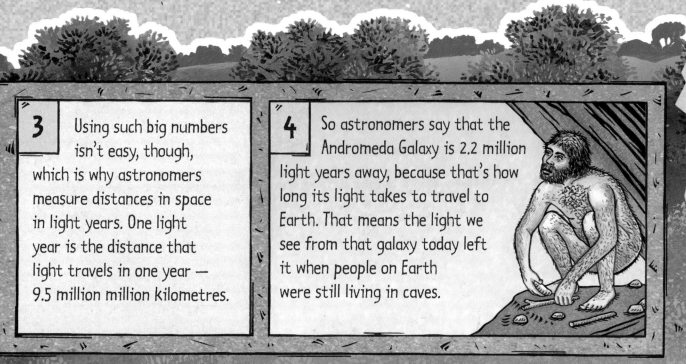

3 Using such big numbers isn't easy, though, which is why astronomers measure distances in space in light years. One light year is the distance that light travels in one year — 9.5 million million kilometres.

4 So astronomers say that the Andromeda Galaxy is 2.2 million light years away, because that's how long its light takes to travel to Earth. That means the light we see from that galaxy today left it when people on Earth were still living in caves.

MEASURING THE UNIVERSE 7

EYE ON THE SKY

1 The universe is so big, and the stars are so far away, that we can see very little just with our eyes.

2 One way of looking at distant objects is to use a telescope. And the bigger the telescope, the further you can see.

3 That's why astronomers use enormous telescopes. This one near Coonabarabran in Australia, has to be kept in a building the size of a seven-storey block of flats.

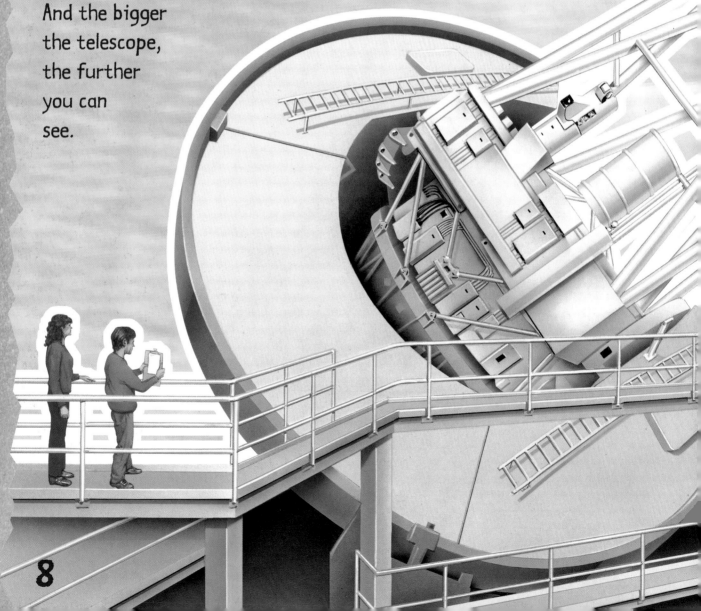

4 But astronomers don't actually look through big telescopes. Instead, everything a big telescope sees is stored inside a computer.

5 The information can be displayed on a screen whenever someone wants to look at it. This means astronomers can get to bed, while their telescopes keep an eye on the night sky!

1 Large telescopes are kept in special buildings called observatories. These have roofs that slide open to reveal the stars.

2 But a telescope can only see the stars if there are no clouds in the way. That's why most observatories are built on the top of high mountains — above the clouds.

3 Yet even on mountaintops, tiny drops of water, dust, and the moving air affect what a telescope sees.

4 So to get the best possible view of the stars and the planets, astronomers have to send telescopes out where there is no air to spoil things — into space!

PULLING POWER

1 Astronomers use telescopes to look for other things in space, besides stars and planets.

2 Black holes are among their most mysterious discoveries — and that's because they're completely invisible.

4 When a star gets close to a black hole, the hole tugs at the star so strongly that it pulls the star's gases away.

3 Although astronomers can't see black holes, they can certainly look at what they do.

1 It's the force called gravity that gives a black hole its super-strong pulling power. Everything in the universe has gravity, and the more massive the object, the stronger its gravity.

2 Luckily for us, the Sun's gravity is powerful enough to keep the planets from drifting off into space — but not so strong that it pulls them into its fiery heat!

10 BLACK HOLES

5 The star's glowing gases swirl around the edge of the hole before disappearing down it for ever.

6 It's the swirling gases from the captured star that astronomers watch. But no one knows what goes on inside the hole itself, because it's far too dark there to see!

3 A black hole's gravity is one of the most powerful things in the universe, sucking in anything that gets too close. Even light can't escape its deadly pull. And since we can't see without light, black holes are invisible.

4 But the really scary thing about a black hole is that every time it swallows something, it gets more massive and its gravity gets stronger. So if you're ever travelling in space remember to steer clear of hungry black holes!

TUNING IN

1 This gigantic telescope is called the Arecibo, and it's on the Caribbean island of Puerto Rico.

2 Stars don't just give out light, they also send out radio signals.

3 And to pick these signals up, astronomers have to use a radio telescope — that's what the Arecibo is.

4 Radio telescopes mean that astronomers don't always have to look for stars, they can listen out for them, too.

12 RADIO TELESCOPES

5 And this means that they can sometimes hear stars whose light is too faint to be seen from Earth.

6 Like satellite dishes, radio telescopes use a dish to collect signals. And the bigger the dish, the more radio signals it can collect.

7 At around 300 metres across, the Arecibo dish is as long as three football pitches. In fact, it's the biggest dish in the world!

1 The Arecibo telescope isn't only used for listening to stars. It's also used to listen out for messages — from aliens!

2 There's no man in the Moon, of course, and we haven't found life on any other planet in our Solar System. So, messages would have to come from planets that belong to distant stars.

3 The Arecibo has also sent out a message, explaining who and where we are. So far there's been no reply, but astronomers are still waiting.

4 Of course, even if we do discover alien life forms, they probably won't look anything like us. We can only hope that they'll be friendly!

DOWN TO EARTH

1 As well as searching for things in space, astronomers try to discover what they're made of.

2 Millions of mini-planets called asteroids travel around the Sun, between the planets Mars and Jupiter.

3 Pebble-sized pieces of asteroid sometimes move away and crash-land on Earth. By studying these space rocks, astronomers have discovered that asteroids are as old as our planet.

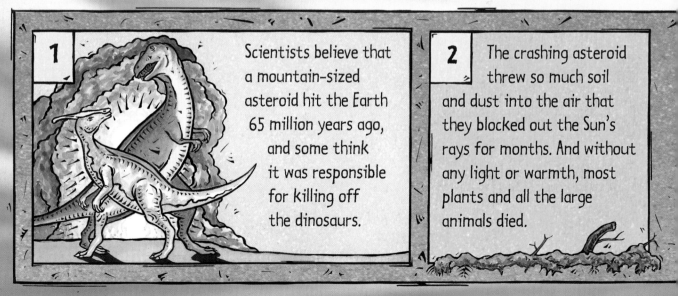

1 Scientists believe that a mountain-sized asteroid hit the Earth 65 million years ago, and some think it was responsible for killing off the dinosaurs.

2 The crashing asteroid threw so much soil and dust into the air that they blocked out the Sun's rays for months. And without any light or warmth, most plants and all the large animals died.

14 ASTEROIDS

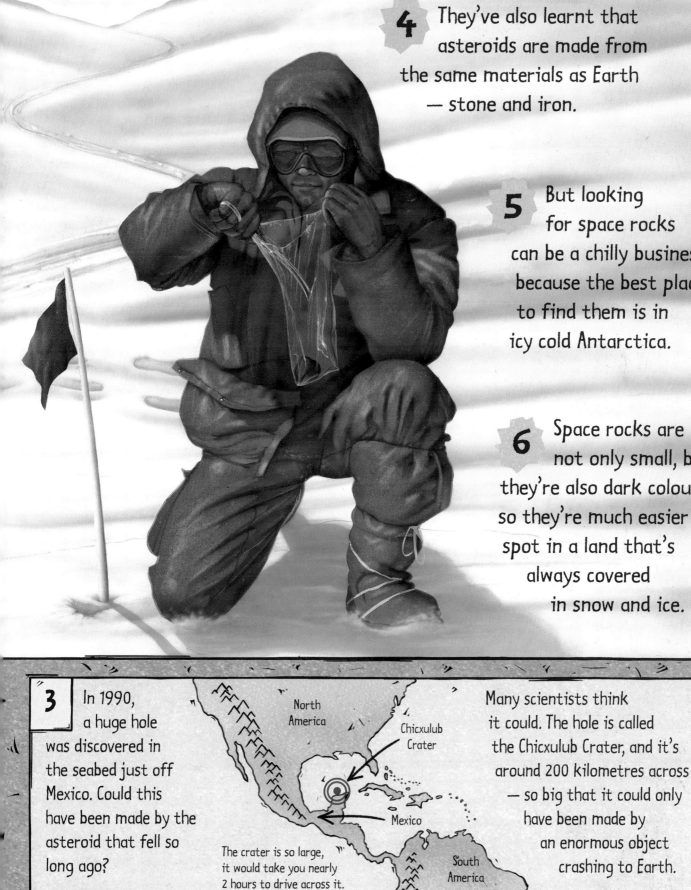

4 They've also learnt that asteroids are made from the same materials as Earth — stone and iron.

5 But looking for space rocks can be a chilly business, because the best place to find them is in icy cold Antarctica.

6 Space rocks are not only small, but they're also dark coloured, so they're much easier to spot in a land that's always covered in snow and ice.

3 In 1990, a huge hole was discovered in the seabed just off Mexico. Could this have been made by the asteroid that fell so long ago?

North America

Chicxulub Crater

Mexico

The crater is so large, it would take you nearly 2 hours to drive across it.

South America

Many scientists think it could. The hole is called the Chicxulub Crater, and it's around 200 kilometres across — so big that it could only have been made by an enormous object crashing to Earth.

MAN ON THE MOON

1 To find out more about our Solar System, scientists need to travel much further than Antarctica. They need to go into space itself!

2 People who travel into space are called astronauts and, so far, the furthest any astronauts have been to is the Moon.

3 But travelling in space is difficult and expensive, and people have to be specially trained to go there.

4 Astronauts have explored the Moon's surface and carried out lots of experiments there. They've also brought back around 380 kilogrammes of Moon rock for astronomers to study.

16 THE MOON

5 Working on the Moon is nothing like being on Earth — for one thing, there's no air to breathe.

6 So astronauts need to take air tanks with them and wear special clothing. Sometimes they even have a special car, like this Moon rover.

1 The first astronauts to visit the Moon landed there on 20 July 1969. While one astronaut, Michael Collins, circled around the Moon in the main spacecraft...

2 ...two others landed in a smaller craft and spent two-and-a-half hours walking about on the surface. The Moon-walkers were called Neil Armstrong and Buzz Aldrin.

3 The astronauts collected two suitcase loads of soil and rock samples for scientists back on Earth to study. They also took close-up photographs of the Moon's surface.

4 When the three arrived home they were greeted by enormous crowds. About 700 million people worldwide had watched the astronauts on television — they were the most famous men in the world!

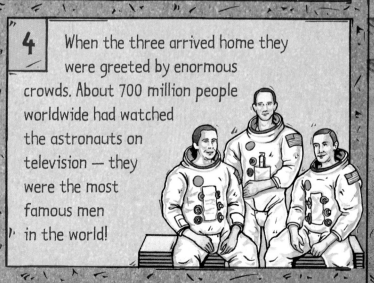

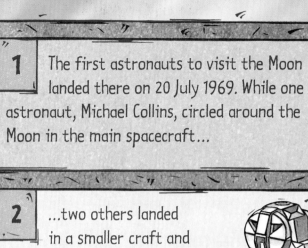

PROBING DEEPER

1 So far, astronauts have only travelled as far as the Moon. But machines called space probes have been much further!

2 Unlike astronauts, probes don't need food, air or sleep. This means they're ideal for sending to planets and moons millions of kilometres away.

3 This robot is called Sojourner. It's the size of a microwave oven, and it's exploring part of the planet Mars. It travelled there on the Pathfinder space probe.

18 SPACE PROBES

4 Pathfinder was launched from Earth by a space rocket in 1996 and reached Mars on 4 July 1997. As it fell towards Mars, Pathfinder was slowed by parachutes, and surrounded by air bags for a soft landing.

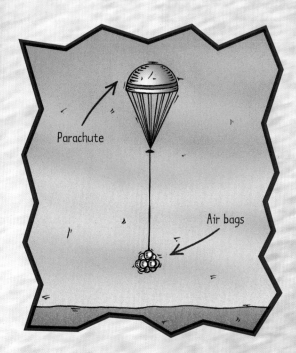

Parachute

Air bags

5 Once the air bags had gone down, Pathfinder opened up and Sojourner moved off. It tested rock and soil samples and sent the information back to Earth.

1 Not all space probes are designed to land on planets. Some probes just fly around them, beaming information back to Earth.

2 The Galileo probe was launched from Earth by the Space Shuttle in 1989. Galileo then set off to study the weather and temperature on the planet Venus.

3 Next, the probe travelled to Jupiter, getting there in 1995. Then, it began its four-year mission to study Jupiter and its four largest moons — Europa, Ganymede, Io, and Callisto.

4 New probes are always being sent into space. Cassini was launched in 1997 to investigate the planet Saturn. Don't hold your breath for the results, though — it won't arrive until the year 2004!

1 Space probes take around a year to reach Mars, the first planet we hope to visit. So if astronauts are ever to travel further than the Moon, we need to know whether it's possible for them to stay in space for such a long time.

2

Mir is a huge Russian space station which travels around the Earth, 400 kilometres above our heads. Astronauts live on board Mir for anything from a few weeks to a year, carrying out experiments to see what living in space is like.

3 One of the strangest things about being on a space station is that you're weightless. Gravity doesn't hold you down, so you float about like a balloon.

4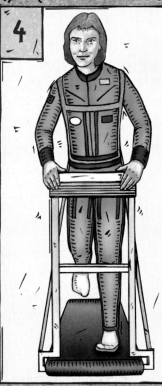

This may sound like fun, but it doesn't do much for your body. Your muscles don't have to work so hard because you're so light, and you have to exercise every day to keep them strong. Of course, you need to be strapped into the exercise machine!

5 Knowing what will happen to our bodies in space will help us to prepare for longer and longer journeys. Maybe one day people will be able to spend their whole lives out in space — exploring the universe for themselves.

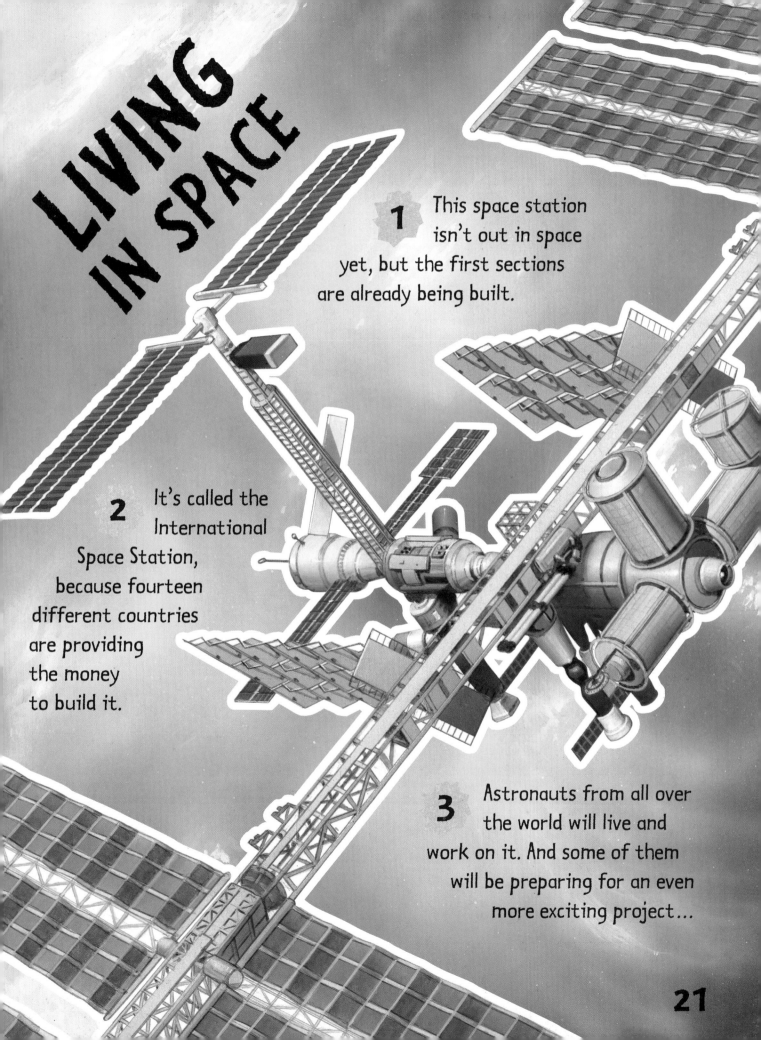

LIVING IN SPACE

1 This space station isn't out in space yet, but the first sections are already being built.

2 It's called the International Space Station, because fourteen different countries are providing the money to build it.

3 Astronauts from all over the world will live and work on it. And some of them will be preparing for an even more exciting project...

21

4 ...building a base on the planet Mars!

5 There are no trees or plants on Mars, of course. So most of the building materials will have to be sent from Earth.

6 Greenhouses will be built, so plants can be grown for food. And although there isn't any oxygen for breathing on Mars, the plants will help to keep the air fresh inside the buildings.

7 That's because people breathe in oxygen and breathe out carbon dioxide gas. And plants take in the carbon dioxide gas and use it to make oxygen.

22 SPACE BASES

8 Water would have to be brought from Earth and every drop recycled so it can be used again and again — even waste water from the toilets!

9 Big radio dishes will keep the base in contact with Earth, while solar panels will turn sunlight into electricity.

10 But who would want to live on another planet? Well, wouldn't you find exploring a distant world exciting?

11 And space explorers would be able to use it as a base for other journeys — even deeper into the universe!

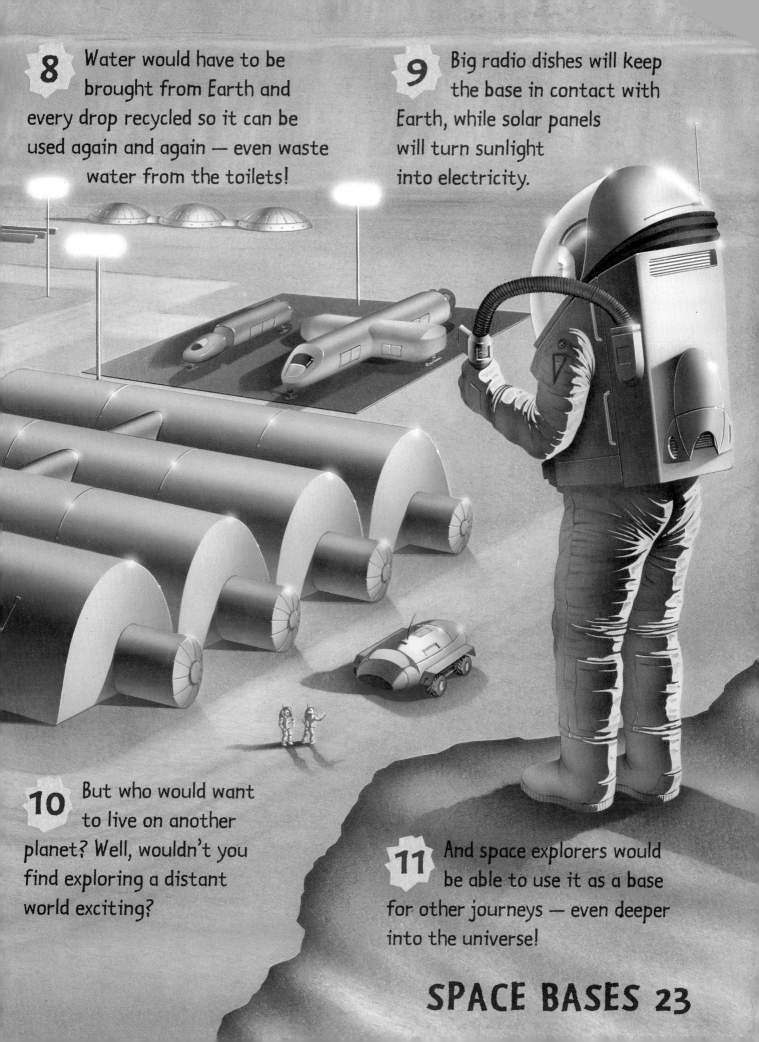

SPACE BASES **23**

INDEX

Main illustrations by Chris Forsey (6-7); Roger Goode (cover, 8-9, 18-19); Christian Hook (21);
Darren Pattenden (14-15); Peter Visscher (12-13); Ian Thompson (title page, 3-5, 10-11, 16-17, 22-23).
Inset and picture-strip illustrations by Ian Thompson.
Thanks to Claire Llewellyn and Beehive Illustration.
Designed by Tiffany Leeson, and edited by Paul Harrison.
Consultant: James Muirden
First published 1998 by Walker Books Ltd, 87 Vauxhall Walk, London SE11 5HJ
2 4 6 8 10 9 7 5 3 1
Text © 1998 Carole Stott
Illustrations © 1998 Walker Books Ltd
This book was typeset in Kosmik.
Printed in Hong Kong
British Library Cataloguing in Publication Data
A catalogue record for this book is available from the British Library.
ISBN 0-7445-2897-6 (Hardback)
ISBN 0-7445-6089-6 (Paperback)

QUIZ ANSWERS

Page 2 — TRUE
Most astronomers believe that the universe will still be growing in millions of years time. Some astronomers think it will then start to shrink until it is too small to see. This is called the Big Crunch.

Page 7 — TRUE
The colour of a star tells us how hot it is. Blue stars are the hottest and red stars are the coolest.

Page 8 — FALSE
Special telescopes are used during the day to take photographs of the Sun.

Page 10 — FALSE
Some astronomers think that there are black holes as small as a pinpoint.

Page 12 — TRUE
TV signals travel deep into space. The oldest TV programmes are around 60 light years away from Earth, now.

Page 14 — TRUE
Over 5,000 of the biggest asteroids have been given names — usually in honour of astronomers, or other famous people. One is even called Santa!

Page 16 — FALSE
Only 12 people have walked on the Moon.

Page 18 — FALSE
When a probe's work is done, it is switched off by remote-control. It is then left to speed through space for ever.

Page 20 — FALSE
Weightlessness means that dust can't settle inside spacecraft. There's so much dust floating around that astronauts sneeze as often as 100 times a day.